AN ADV

ABIDE
WITH US

Devotionals, Meditations, and
Candle Lighting Services
for Advent & the 12 Days of Christmas

Prepared by pastors in regional ministry
in the Christian Church (Disciples of Christ)
Bilingual candlelight devotions are
provided by leaders in Obra Hispana

Rev. Dr. Paul B. Koch, editor

chalice
PRESS

This book was edited by Paul Koch and bi-lingual candlelight devotions were provided by leaders in Obra Hispana.

Print: 9780827245006
EPUB: 9780827245013
EPDF: 9780827245020

ChalicePress.com

Printed in the United States of America

Table of Contents

Introduction

Greetings, beloved! The Holy Seasons of Advent and Christmas reflect the hopes, goodwill, compassion, expectations, and joys we voice every day of the year in our lives of discipleship. I and other members of the College of Regional Ministers collaborate to celebrate what is fundamental in our faith and offer our best to you – from the first possible date of Advent to Epiphany.

Concluding a most beloved carol, *O Little Town of Bethlehem*, Phillips Brooks writes: *"O come to us, **abide with us**, our God, Emmanuel."* His plea is essentially Emmanuel's name – Abide with Us, God with us. God is here in Jesus Christ!

To abide means to be present but conveys a softer tone. A further definition is poetic, "to continue without fading or being lost." Sometimes our light and all that shines from within fades. Trials and travails mute our brilliance. We also can lose our bearings in where we stand or what we believe – we can be lost. The Good News of Jesus Christ, Emmanuel – God with us, is that Jesus is by our side even in settings of loss. He is Abiding with us!

Thank you for sharing in this special discipline of reading scripture, devotion, and prayer each day with all of us in local, regional, general, lay, non-congregationally based, constituent, and chaplaincy ministry. We abide together!

— Rev. Teresa "Terri" Hord Owens

Witnesses to the Light

John 1

John was not the light; he came only as a witness to the light.
— John 1:8

I recently listened to a leading edge Atheist, and what I didn't see in this man making his argument logically against the reality of God was....Light. He was pushing the upper limits of what we can understand on our own with our human resources. And no light. 'The people walking in darkness have seen a great light.'

I liken our lives to a candle. The candle is nice to look at, but its sole purpose is to share light. How many of us go through life looking good on the outside but our candle isn't burning, we have no light to share? Jesus said, "I am the light of the world," but he also said to those who received him, "you are the light of the world, so let your light shine."

This is the Christmas message we learn from John--we are called to be Witnesses to the Light! May it shine brightly in our hearts this Advent as we light one another's candles to remind us of this great truth!

O coming Light, let us dwell you in and realize how much one single candle flame, one Light can dispel all darkness.

— Rev. Ron Routledge

Christmas with Mark

Mark 1

The beginning of the good news about Jesus the Messiah...
— Mark 1:1

Star. Angels. Shepherds. Census. Manger. Magi. Gold. Frankincense. Myrrh. These raw elements we call, "the Christmas story." Two Christmas stories – told by Matthew and Luke. Both writers tell in their own way the story of the incarnation, the coming of Christ into our broken world.

I am fascinated that the first gospel written doesn't include a birth story. Mark starts with grown-up Jesus asking John to baptize him for remission of sins. Mark seemingly has no need for hype, to claim that prophets predicted his birth, that angels or magi celebrated it. Mark doesn't claim that Jesus was born without sin. Mark seems happy for Jesus to just be human, born like us. The first thing Mark tells us: Jesus asked to be baptized for the remission of sins. Remarkable.

It's miracle enough when one human being puts aside the need to be better than, overcomes the temptation to resort to violence, doesn't worry about whether he's hanging out with "the cool kids," but just loves every single person he meets. Even without the manger, that's a beautiful Christmas message!

God of light and life, we celebrate the mystery of your presence, wisdom, and steadfast love for us and all Creation.

— Rev. Dr. Jay R. Hartley

Tear Open the Heavens

Isaiah 64:1-9

If only you would tear open the heavens and come down!
— Isaiah 64:1

Advent is a time of active waiting. But what exactly are we waiting for? Are we waiting for God to tear open the heavens and come down: to raise the valleys, lower the hills, and straighten the curves.

I remember Eugene Peterson paraphrasing John 1 in *The Message.* "The word became flesh and bone and moved into the neighborhood." Is this what we're waiting for, for Emmanuel to be born in us? Are we waiting for God to bust down the doors and set everything right?

I can't help but wonder if I've been coming at this the wrong way all these years. What would it look like, if instead of *us* asking *God* to move in with us and be roommates, *we* answered God's flyer requesting a co-habitant?

This Advent season, let us endeavor to move in with God: move into the neighborhoods where God is living; the school districts where God is teaching; the shelters, pantries, encampments where God is living. After all, what if it is God who is saying to us, "Abide with me"?

O Lord, help us to meet you where you are this Advent season. Help us to abide with you!

— Rev. David Woodard

Ordinary People and the Revelation of God

Luke 1—2; Matthew 2:1-12

Zechariah asked the angel, "How can I be sure of this? I am an old man and my wife is well along in years." The angel said to him, "I am Gabriel. I stand in the presence of God, and I have been sent to speak to you and to tell you this good news." — Luke 1:18-19

Between the Old and New Testament, God's voice was silent. Then when God was ready, God's voice was heard and actions revealed. The revelation of God was placed in the hands of ordinary people to display God's love as the remedy of life's disappointments, pain, and despair. The New Testament begins with a shift in how God reveals Godself and speaks into human life. Instead of powerful prophets of notable backgrounds, God used Mary, a teenager; Joseph, a working-class man; shepherds as service workers; unnamed angels; Elizabeth, an old, barren woman, and Zechariah, an older adult, wise men from foreign lands; and a baby born without an address. Without hesitation, these ordinary people offered themselves to reveal the voice and actions of God.

What about you? Can we offer ourselves this Advent season as ordinary people to reveal the voice and actions of God in a world that needs the hope, peace, joy, and love that comes from Christ? Can we tell the story of Jesus Christ in our lives so that some person traveling through life can hear the voice of God in a new way and come to trust and surrender their life to God?

God, Let's do it; let's do it together!

— Rev. Dr. Denise Bell

Wondering and Wandering

Psalm 8:3-4 (MSG)

I look up at your macro-skies, dark and enormous,
your handmade sky-jewelry,
Moon and stars mounted in their settings.
Then I look at my micro-self and wonder,
Why do you bother with us?
Why take a second look our way?
— Psalm 8:3-4 (MSG)

Advent and Lent share the liturgical color purple. Both hearken darkness as a gift to understand the coming light of Christmas and Easter. Seasons of *special time* are intimately connected.

I went to a funeral during the heat of summer and we sang the favorite hymn of the deceased, *I Wonder as I Wander*. I was startled as it is a Christmas carol – opposite time of year; opposite purpose…. Yet the mournful words and the Appalachian melody spoke to me. *"…out under the sky, how Jesus the Savior did come for to die for poor ordinary people like you and like I."*

Psalm 8 reads: "I look up at our macro-skies, dark and enormous, your handmade sky-jewelry, moon and stars mounted in their setting. Then I look at my micro-self and wonder, Why do you bother with us? Why take a second look our way?" Wandering isn't encouraged in other aspects of religion; mystery is replaced by certainty. Bless that honest pilgrim singing in the night.

I encourage you to sing carols at all times of year for a devotional (wondering) practice. What new meanings might wander your way?

High from God's heaven, may a star's light fall, so the promise of ages
I can recall.

— Rev. Dr. Paul Koch

More Nostalgia and Less Bible?

Matthew 1:1–17

This is the genealogy of Jesus the Messiah the son of David, the son of Abraham:... Thus there were fourteen generations in all from Abraham to David, fourteen from David to the exile to Babylon, and fourteen from the exile to the Messiah." — Matthew 1:1, 17

As Christmas draws near, my heart grows more nostalgic. I'm reminded of beloved traditions from childhood: decorating the Christmas tree the day after Thanksgiving, keeping up with a daily Advent calendar to mark the days leading up to Christmas, attending candlelight Christmas Eve worship with family, gathering around the warm fire at my grandparent's home to open presents on Christmas Day.

I'm also learning that I need to guard against some aspects of nostalgia, especially when it comes to the deepest import of the Christmas stories. For as much as I love the Christmas memories of my childhood, few of them connect with the more radical implications of the gospel, including the genealogy of Jesus, which consisted of numerous women who defied societal expectations to such a degree that without their persistence, history never would've heard a word from Jesus. Indeed, if our Christmas remembrances don't include stories about the subversive power of women alongside the figure of Christ, we have to wonder if we are recalling more nostalgia and less Bible.

Mothering God, open our hearts to the fullness of the gospel this Advent season, so that we might celebrate all the people — including all the women — who make your story possible.

— Rev. Dr. Phil Snider

Tradition vs New Things

Isaiah 43:18-19

"Forget the former things;
do not dwell on the past.
See, I am doing a new thing!
Now it springs up; do you not perceive it?
I am making a way in the wilderness
and streams in the wasteland."
— Isaiah 43:18-19

Two favorite Christmas carols are "Little Drummer Boy" and "Do You Hear What I Hear?" Advent asks the same questions. What will we bring to the soon-to-arrive Jesus?

We prepare to receive Jesus again, to deepen our relationships, seek meaning, reflection, and growth. God offers God's best to each of us in Jesus. Grace, mercy, and love for all. We must decide if we will offer our best to God through Jesus. We commit to work and grow our spirits as we seek God.

Isaiah reminds that God always God calls us. He asks us to forget the former things and look to what God is doing now! It's a challenge to lay down what we know, expect, and understand and come to Jesus like a child as Matthew asks us to do. What do I need to lay down so that I can better serve and love in the coming year?

Advent is an amazing season of change, challenge, growth, and tradition. God asks us to walk into this season willing to take a chance and grow. How will you answer?

God, help what will I lay down this season so I can be the follower of Jesus that God wants me this coming year.

— Rev. Tom Stanley

Anticipation

Micah 4:1-5

...They will beat their swords into plowshares
and their spears into pruning hooks...
and no one will make them afraid,
for the Lord Almighty has spoken...
— Micah 4:3-4

Advent is the season of already-but not yet. It is a season of anticipation, of waiting, in which we remember the promises made and look forward longingly to the time when those promises are fulfilled. This passage from the prophet Micah paints an image of a time and place where people live in harmony with one another in peace and safety. It is an image of God's dream for humankind, a vision not yet fulfilled. We are still waiting. But it need not be a season of passive waiting. As we consider this vision that Micah lays out for us, in this season of anticipation, we are invited to wonder how we can move the vision forward. How can we partner with God to prepare the soil and plant the seeds for the peace that Micah imagines? How can God use us to create moments of wholeness, opportunities for reconciliation, spaces for hope? May God make us instruments of God's peace.

God of grace, in this time of waiting, use us to help your dreams of peace come true.

— Rev. Sandy Messick

Endowed Encounters

Colossians 1:15-20

The Son is the image of the invisible God, the firstborn over all creation. For in him all things were created: things in heaven and on earth, visible and invisible, whether thrones or powers or rulers or authorities; all things have been created through him and for him. He is before all things, and in him all things hold together.
— *Colossians 1:15-17*

Today's lesson is fully endowed with the total Christ-story from creation to the cross, and includes a hymn that shapes the liturgy of our daily walk with God. There is praise, adoration, attribution and hoped for (not to mention boldly and lovingly accomplished) peace in this sacred text. It is a beautiful hymn of the season that has the inspiration embedded within to lift the church and each member of the body to new heights of praise and proclamation.

Embedded within the sacred text of our hearts, too, is inspiration to lift high our heads in praise and proclamation. Just as we celebrate the truth of the incarnation of God with us, we are enlisted and assigned by virtue of our baptism to be an incarnate people who carry and share the very real presence and peace of God into this day. Today we may encounter one who is feeling untethered, disconnected, broken, irreconcilable and lacking any sense of the peace that passes all understanding. Be awake and watch for this one; remember that the gospel good news is that within us is a hymn to be shared with God's precious ones.

May our hymn of praise and love be shared with all we meet.

— Rev. Thaddaeus B. Allen

A Passage for Advent and Lent

Isaiah 58:6–11

Then your light will break forth like the dawn,
and your healing will quickly appear;
then your righteousness[J] will go before you,
and the glory of the Lord will be your rear guard.
Then you will call, and the Lord will answer;
you will cry for help, and he will say: Here am I.
— Isaiah 58:8-9

Cold weather, shorter days, and longer nights tempt us to reduce peace to tranquility. Say, "Peace," and people conjure images of a soft glow of candlelight, good friends and family, meat, cheese, starchy sides, chocolate, and soft music. I like tranquility too, but does this match the biblical vision of peace?

We often read Isaiah 58:6-11 at Lent rather than Advent. Yet, both seasons are meant to serve the same purpose—to reorient our spiritual and ethical lives. Peace in Isaiah is physical security for all people--not just some. Security found in knowing and trusting our neighbors and being people they also can trust. Peace is an end to hunger, thirst, injustice, and exclusion. Peace means everyone has a home. So just as Lent gives us space to examen our lives, Advent also prompts prayers of examen.

Have I acted as though my suffering makes me a helpless victim while someone else's suffering is probably their own fault? Have I wanted to see people punished more than I desire to see them repent? Have I become calloused to other's suffering because they do not look or act like me? Have I convinced myself that force will keep me safe?

— Rev. Andy Mangum

All Means All

Isaiah 64:1–9

Yet you, Lord, are our Father.
We are the clay, you are the potter;
we are all the work of your hand.
— Isaiah 64:8 (The Message)

The Big Bang Theory is a scientific explanation for how the universe began. Simply put, it says the universe began when an infinitely dense single point, smaller than the tip of a needle, inflated within a millisecond, releasing a vast array of fundamental particles such as neutrons, electrons and protons. These were the raw materials, the "star dust", that are the building blocks for everything that exists in the today's 13.7-billion-year-old universe.

If you accept the Big Bang Theory and if you accept Isaiah's metaphor of God as our potter, then the metaphorical clay from which we each are formed is the "star dust" that has been in existence from the very beginning. Far from being the angry God envisioned by Isaiah, God has proven to be a loving potter, a God who would "open the heavens and descend" to "abide with us" in the form of a human baby made from the same "star dust" infused clay as the rest of us.

It may be difficult to fully understand the momentous "Big Bang" event. But it is easy to understand the even more momentous advent of the potter's love made manifest in the Christ Child. Amen.

— Rev. Bill Robey

THURSDAY

Great Joy

Matthew 2:10

When they saw the star, they were overjoyed.
— Matthew 2:10

Magi entered a season of joyful anticipation when they saw that unique star in the east. It was not stationary, they had to follow it and when it stopped over the place where the child was, the Magi rejoiced. Their season of anticipation had concluded, the Christ child had been found. They entered in, worshiped him, and presented him their gifts.

The caustic divisiveness permeating our country causes great anxiety in this Advent season, but don't let it steal our joy. Quoting Craddock: "Take a saint, and put him in any condition, and he knows how to rejoice in the Lord."

We gather with family and friends and utilize technology to capture the joy and happiness of their presence. Christmas worship will be time of the festive singing of carols and rejoicing anew at the birth of our Lord and Savior. The presence of the Holy Spirit manifests the power of words sung and spoken. "Joy to the world the Lord has come. Let earth receive her King."

May our experience this season be filled with joy and gladness as we give Christ the same reverence as did the Magi when they gave their gifts. Shalom.

— Rev. Dr. Eugene James

From Where Will My Help Come?

Psalm 121

I lift up my eyes to the mountains—
where does my help come from?
My help comes from the Lord,
the Maker of heaven and earth.
— Psalm 121:1-2

In his book "Churches and the Crisis of Decline: A Hopeful, Practical Ecclesiology for a Secular Age," Andrew Root tells an alternative story for a church that closed. It is an invitation to imagine "a way where there is no way," not based on innovation, or a magical young leader, but on seeking God's way for the life of this church.

The story starts with wisdom shared by a recently deceased grandmother to her grandson. She told him that he needed three things for a good life. The first two: "Take care of your teeth and Save some money." He goes to her church Bible study and asks them for help with the third, "Can you help me Find God?"

"Can we?" The quest stirs memory of how "God had found them."

In this season of Advent, I wonder if we might be stirred to remember how God has made a way for us, when there was no way? I wonder if we might seek our help not in what we can do, but in what God has done and is doing?

O Christ, help us to be open to finding You.

— Rev. Dr. Teresa Dulyea-Parker

Peace Amid Chaos

Psalm 85:8

I will listen to what God the Lord says;
he promises peace to his people, his faithful servants—
but let them not turn to folly.
— Psalm 85:8

Peace seems far from us. Around the world and close to home, there is the threat of violence – at work, in communities, schools, families, and even in churches. Some wonder if God intended dissension. God has offered forgiveness and restoration in the past and God offers peace and salvation again!

Are you listening for God to speak peace in the midst of anger and disagreements that surround you? Do you recognize words of love from God addressing the anxiety and guilt within you? If you recognize words of peace from God, what happens to them?

This season, give voice to the deep longings through faith – for hope, peace, joy, love, and light – which stand in stark contrast to the brokenness and discord in us and around us. I wonder if this season is an opportunity for us to hear what God is speaking into our lives *and* to make those things part of our lives. I wonder if God's words of peace do not simply come into the world around us, but also in us and through us.

Gracious God, ease the anger and chaos around me and within me.
Speak peace into my life and into the lives of others through my life.

— Rev. Joshua Patty

God's Loving Response to Pain

Isaiah 40:1–11

Comfort, comfort my people,
says your God.
— Isaiah 40:1

For many, it is impossible to read Isaiah 40 without hearing Handel's *Messiah*: "Comfort ye, Comfort ye my people." Handel's setting of this scripture is gentle, peaceful, soothing. One imagines a parent wrapping their arms around a hurting child.

Soothing music is necessary if there has been pain. So many of our great stories of faith are in response to pain and suffering. The birth of Samuel – God's loving response to Hannah's suffering. The Exodus – God's loving response to the pain under a cruel pharaoh. And these words from Isaiah 40 – God's loving response to living in exile.

The power of the Christian faith is rooted in God's loving response to our pain. If we put on a happy face when we go to church, if we pretend like everything is okay, if we decorate and dress up and sing carols but gloss over the reality of pain, we miss what Christ offers us: comfort, renewal, hope. Christ comes to us in our suffering, acknowledges our pain, and loves us into healing. Thanks be to God!

God of mercy and compassion, we thank you for your steadfast love
which brings us through pain and offers hope for new life.

— Rev. Dr. Jay R. Hartley

A Season for Preparation

Galatians 6:2

Carry each other's burdens, and in this way you will fulfill the law of Christ.
— Galatians 6:2

As the winter days grow shorter, the nights grow longer and colder on our farm making it more difficult for the animals to survive on their own. When the grass is gone and the ponds frozen, they will suffer or perish if we don't prepare ahead and provide life-sustaining elements.

As the Advent preparation days grow shorter and the nights grow longer, fellow travelers wander in the cold and darkness, carrying heavy burdens of life, loneliness, hunger, uncertainty, in need of compassion. Paul tells us in Galatians to bear another's burden, to lighten their load, to connect and be present with kindness, generosity, and goodwill. What better time than now to reach out with Christ's love, bringing light into their darkness.

As we prepare and reflect through this Advent season, the coming of Christ, let us not forget what God has done for us and the needs of this world. We are called to be Christ's hands and feet in this broken world providing life sustaining elements, for both physical and emotional wellbeing for our neighbors who need the Hope, Peace, Joy and Love we proclaim.

Lord, open our eyes, our ears, our hearts to the needs of the world and wisdom to make a difference.

— Rev. Jennifer Long

Clarity in Verse Four

Luke 2:8-11

And there were shepherds living out in the fields nearby, keeping watch over their flocks at night. An angel of the Lord appeared to them, and the glory of the Lord shone around them, and they were terrified. But the angel said to them, "Do not be afraid. I bring you good news that will cause great joy for all the people. Today in the town of David a Savior has been born to you; he is the Messiah, the Lord." — Luke 2:8-11

Written in 1849, *It Came Upon the Midnight Clear* was one of the first carols composed by American Edmund Sears. When I was a parish minister, I occasionally had to work with the choir director to get the fourth verse sung; it was too somber and down for such a "happy season:"

And you, beneath life's crushing load
Whose forms are bending low;
Who toil along the climbing way
With painful steps and slow -

Look now, for glad and golden hours
Come swiftly on the wing.
Oh, rest beside the weary road,
And hear the angels sing.

For many, the Advent season contains hard days, and I take great comfort in his words. We may not have the time, money, or opportunity to run away for a self-care day. We may not have the chance to get off the 'weary road,' even for a short detour. Sears reminds us that it can be enough to simply rest where we are – before the cantata rehearsal, during the family dinner, while we are surrounded by shoppers in a crowded mall – and listen to good tidings of great joy.

Listen.

Dear God, may our somber fourth verses in life add to the clarity of those we want to memorize.

— Rev. Molly Smothers

Bethlehem Perspectives I

Micah 5:1–5, Luke 21:34–38

"But you, Bethlehem Ephrathah,
though you are small among the clans[J] of Judah,
out of you will come for me
one who will be ruler over Israel,
whose origins are from of old,
from ancient times."
— Micah 5:2

What on earth was Micah suggesting? Writing to the Nation of Israel, probably after Israel returned from Exile, Micah specifically names a small town in Judah called Bethlehem Ephrathah – the birthplace of Jesus. Bethlehem was also the birthplace of King David. Micah was telling Israel that when "the people return to join the Israelites, he will stand and shepherd his flock" – that is, David will stand and lead the people of Israel.

Next, read Luke 21:34-38, in which Luke tells us that Jesus was at the temple. After entering Jerusalem (20.28) and cleansing the Temple (20.45), Jesus is confronted by Jewish leaders, "...by what authority are you doing these things?"

Let's see if we can connect some dots between these two readings from our Scriptures with life today as we center ourselves in this Season of Lent. There is a line that hangs like a dangling participle that functions more like a warning as Luke declares to us, "Be careful."

Tomorrow, we will see how "being careful" is a reminder of the importance of maintaining strong spiritual practices.

Holy One, let us be mindful of our contexts of being – whether rooted in our town, our church, our Season, our lives....

— Rev. Christopher B. Morton

Bethlehem Perspectives II

Micah 5:1–5, Luke 21:34–38

"Be careful, or your hearts will be weighed down with carousing, drunkenness and the anxieties of life, and that day will close on you suddenly like a trap. For it will come on all those who live on the face of the whole earth. Be always on the watch, and pray that you may be able to escape all that is about to happen, and that you may be able to stand before the Son of Man." — Luke 21:34-36

A line hangs like a dangling participle that functions like a warning, "Be careful." Luke goes on to say "...your hearts will be weighed down with carousing, drunkenness, and the anxieties of life..." (v34) Carousing could be the mischief you stir to distract from present-day difficulties. Drunkenness may not be wine, beer, or distilled spirits but can be food, play, or work. Anxieties are causing us to wander. To claim loyalties to our mischief, to our imbibing in our addictions, and being increasingly disconnected from our inner lights – from the divine within us, as well as seeing the divine in each other. "Be careful!"

Luke reminds a shepherd is already here. Set aside the anxiety-induced choices and turn to the shepherd now. Turn from the bright lights of distraction, and towards your inner light; let your light reflect the hope that you hold for moment, the day, and time to come.

We wander, seeking ways to connect with You, to sit at Your feet, to listen and learn. Since we cannot silence our minds, help us to trust You enough to pause our inner voices so that we might bear witness to Your desires. And claim with Jesus the authority within us.

— Rev. Christopher B. Morton

FRIDAY

A Christmas Story

John 15:7-11

If you remain in me and my words remain in you, ask whatever you wish, and it will be done for you. This is to my Father's glory, that you bear much fruit, showing yourselves to be my disciples. As the Father has loved me, so have I loved you. Now remain in my love. If you keep my commands, you will remain in my love, just as I have kept my Father's commands and remain in his love. I have told you this so that my joy may be in you and that your joy may be complete. — John 15:7-11

I spent time in the mountains of Georgia, celebrating the birthday of a colleague. We attended a Christmas musical and dinner and did not anticipate an ice storm on top of the mountain. The further we climbed, the more ice and snow we encountered, until we could go no further.

The cabin was right around the corner. We could have walked. However, my friend's brother took the wheel and navigated us around the slippery slope. We made it to the other side. And there we were, for the next two days, together yet isolated, comfortable yet anxious, trusting yet uncertain, abiding with one another.

The cabin was spacious enough for everyone to get into their own cubby hole. The homeowner told my friend on the phone, "whatever is in the house, you can have." With games, movies, laughter, and plenty of cooking, we began to know each other in more intimate ways.

We experienced the security of being welcome in a stranger's home. We had food to sustain us until tree branches could be moved from the road. We were grateful.

Thank you for the opportunity to abide with you and each other to spaces of safety and security.

— Rev. Dr. Nadine Burton

God's Anointing Calls Us to Change the World

Isaiah 61:1–4, 8–11

I delight greatly in the Lord;
my soul rejoices in my God.
For he has clothed me with garments of salvation
and arrayed me in a robe of his righteousness....
For as the soil makes the sprout come up
and a garden causes seeds to grow,
so the Sovereign Lord will make righteousness
and praise spring up before all nations.
— Isaiah 61:10-11

We feel a special focus for our lives to think, speak, and act differently because of religious commitments. Through baptism, we are unquestionably called to service in God's name. Some who are called are also anointed by God to a life of intentional service and specific witness.

Isaiah understood a particular calling of the People of God was to speak truth to power and to change the behaviors of the people and restructure religious, social, and political policies and practices that directly affect the people.

For Isaiah, this anointing was life-changing. God's claim upon his life meant very practical and dramatic ways of being and behaving in the world, from bringing good news to the oppressed to repairing ruined cities. Jesus would echo this understanding of anointing as he began his own ministry.

Let us realize that the birth of the infant Jesus isn't simply about warm and fuzzy feelings, but an anointing to a life of profound service to God to change the world for the better.

Anointing God, remind us on our Advent journey to once again prepare
our lives to be fully claimed by you and be ready to change the world
in Jesus' name.

— Rev. Allen V. Harris

Eyes of the Blind Shall Be Opened

Isaiah 35:5–10

They will enter Zion with singing;
everlasting joy will crown their heads.
Gladness and joy will overtake them,
and sorrow and sighing will flee away.
— Isaiah 35:10

Handel's *Messiah* reveals extra meaning when shared through a community sing-a-long. While merry choristers may not be pitch-perfect and are tempo-temperamental, hearts are on-key! "Glory to God, Glory to God in the Highest!"

Many of *Messiah*'s famous choruses are well-known but between each are lesser-known recitatives. Introducing "He Shall Feed His Flock Like a Shepherd" is Isaiah 35:5-10. At a concert, a soprano sang her heart out with so much talent, joy, and enthusiasm, I felt as she did, that "The Eyes of the Blind Shall be Opened…"

On public radio the next day, the announcer was equally captivated by her recitative. They told us about the soprano. She is a noted local singer and jazz pianist - and has been blind since birth. Of course she asked to sing Isaiah's prophecy as she knows firsthand the miracle the Christ child brings. One day all of us shall see clearly and our ears will be unstopped. Waters shall break out in the wilderness and streams in the desert! – beginning with my tears.

May we come to you, O Zion with songs and everlasting joy upon our heads; we shall obtain joy and gladness, and sorrow and sighing shall flee away.

— Rev. Dr. Paul Koch

23

Presence

Luke 1:39–45

When Elizabeth heard Mary's greeting, the baby leaped in her womb, and Elizabeth was filled with the Holy Spirit.
— *Luke 1:41*

My friend was preparing to have her first child and the baby had a heart condition. Because of this, extra people were needed for the delivery. As she labored, the room filled up. Doctors and nurses were there to support the mother as well as the child to be born. As the room began to fill, my friend realized, with the exception of her husband, everyone was female. She said in that moment, she felt a deep connection to herself, to women in all time and places. It was a powerful moment of feeling upheld and supported by other women.

I often think of my friend's experience when I read about Mary visiting Elizabeth. What Mary needed in that moment was the support of someone who deeply knew what was happening in her body and in her spirit. Being known and held is powerful. Presence, abiding with one another, is powerful. The power of the incarnation, of Emmanuel, God with us. Presence – knowing we are upheld, fully connects – may it be so.

Abiding God, as we await the incarnation of your love come to earth, be present in the relationships we share with one another as we support, love, and offer grace to one another.

— Rev. Cheryl Russell Kunkel

TUESDAY

A Song

Luke 1:46-55

Mary said,
"My soul glorifies the Lord
and my spirit rejoices in God my Savior,
for he has been mindful
of the humble state of his servant.
From now on all generations will call me blessed,
for the Mighty One has done great things for me—
holy is his name.
— Luke 1: 46-48

During these weeks of Advent, music that surrounds our lives changes us, brings us closer to the story as we sing of the Little Town of Bethlehem or Away in a Manger. We pause to hear the story anew, pause to bask in the wonder.

Mary's visit with Elizabeth moves Mary to song. She sings a song of revolution, of transformation, of God's love made manifest in the world, a song of praise.

Mary's song invites us to see the world as God sees it.

Not just as it could be, but through the eyes of God's grace and hope.

We are invited to pause and let the uncertainty, despair, and brokenness fall away and let God's vision come into focus.

Pause and dwell here where God's justice is made manifest.

Pause and dwell in the wonder of a love powerful enough to transform.

Pause and dwell in the mystery of God's presence incarnate in the world.

Pause and dwell in the promise of Emmanuel, God with us.

God of presence, infiltrate our lives with your promise of hope, the mystery of your perfect love, your revelation of justice and move us to work for the day when your vision of wholeness comes into focus for all.

— Rev. Cheryl Russell Kunkel

A Balance of Light and Night

Genesis 1:1-5

In the beginning God created the heavens and the earth. Now the earth was formless and empty, darkness was over the surface of the deep, and the Spirit of God was hovering over the waters. And God said, "Let there be light," and there was light. God saw that the light was good, and he separated the light from the darkness. God called the light "day," and the darkness he called "night." And there was evening, and there was morning—the first day. — Genesis 1:1-5

At sunrise, look for the "violet flame" – a spark when the red colors of dawn meet the indigo sky. This brief flash, a healing gift of liminal beauty, merges "the red of conscious perspective with the blue of forgiving love."

When winter solstice arrives, North Americans experience the longest night of the year. More light will shine on faces each day until the summer solstice returns us to a lengthening night. Both are needed!

Most religions harken this time for their greatest faith stories. Christians are in the Dark Wood of Advent, where candles of hope, peace, joy, and love proclaim the coming light. Jews during Chanukah remember a miracle of presence and preservation by lighting eight candles. Hindus celebrate Diwali, a Festival of Lights. Muslims proclaim God as Light. Indigenous societies keep a Sacred Fire for the transition of seasons. We celebrate together!

The colors of Advent and Christmas: violet, gold, red, green, pink, blue… radiate a candleflame. May this longest night be met with warmth and glow. Night cannot be overcome by force or violence, only by lighting one candle at a time.

Radiant Jesus, you arrived in the silence of night, so we can see your great light. Thank you!

— Rev. Dr. Paul Koch

The Hungry Shall be Filled

Luke 1:53

He has filled the hungry with good things and sent the
rich away empty.
— *Luke 1:53 NRSVU*

Have you noticed that the hungry are not filled with *food* but with "good things." The rich are not sent away *empty-handed* or *unfed* but "empty"? While on a solidarity trip to Nicaragua in 1984, a group of us visited a Salvadoran refugee camp populated by those who had escaped death squads - some of whose leaders our country had helped to train and arm in the School of the Americas. As we were about to leave, a grandmother we had met rushed up to the van smiling and insistent, holding up a stack of freshly made corn tortillas to make sure that we had food for the rest of our journey. It was half of the day's supply for her and her extended family – a gracious act of hospitality that became the "bread" for a service of communion that night and painful acknowledgements of emptiness we had not noticed within our privileged selves.

O God, as I prepare for this Christmas, may I ask that You increase
my hunger to live more like Jesus?

— Rev. William B. Rose-Heim

27

Imagine

Luke 1:26-38

Mary was greatly troubled at his words and wondered what kind of greeting this might be…. "How will this be," Mary asked the angel.
— Luke 1:29, 34

Imagine what Mary felt like when told she would give birth to a son. Such news would be scary, embarrassing, and shameful for the family, it was a death sentence. Not only that, this comes from a stranger that was babbling about how she was favored by God and that this child, called the "Son of the Most High" would assume the throne of their ancestor David. If you were Mary, wouldn't you be more than a little skeptical?

Have we not experienced times when we have been confronted with a life situation that seemed so overwhelming, so frightening that all we have wanted to do is run away? In such times what eases our anxiety?

Mary is given the assurance she will have the help of the Holy Spirit. She is told God is at work in other people's lives that are connected to her story, and she is reminded that with God's help there is nothing that is impossible. Perhaps this is the message God has for us in this text, and that in all things, God asks of us is to surrender our will and our lives to the leading of the Spirit.

Immanuel, what personal will might I surrender to follow in your Spirit.

— Rev. Ken Marston

Love Came Down

John 1:1-4

In the beginning was the Word, and the Word was with God, and the Word was God. He was with God in the beginning. Through him all things were made; without him nothing was made that has been made. In him was life, and that life was the light of all mankind. Who can explain love? If it was up to us, we would only love those who love us, forgive those who forgive us, be faithful to those who were faithful to us. But God's love is unreasonable and just when I believe I have grasped it, it makes me look again. — John 1:1-4

I am amazed that God chose to enter into a covenant of love with us, a covenant that does not depend on our faithfulness, but on the faithfulness of God.

But God has come; and God is with us and the end is written. We hold the waiting for a world that so desperately needs saving. We hold the promise on behalf of those who feel forsaken, and for ourselves in our own forsakenness. But when the time had fully come, God sent Jesus and love came down.

- **Love** came when the time was right.
- **Love** came to the right people
- **Love is** overwhelming - no matter what happens in life, struggles I must face, what others might say or do nor the trial or test I'm loved.

Lord, please help me to remember that you loved me so much that you brought your love and light down to reconcile us back to yourself.

— Rev. Dr. Don K. Gillett II

Abide with Us

Matthew 1:23

"The virgin will conceive and give birth to a son, and they will call him Immanuel" (which means "God with us").
— *Matthew 1:23*

Emmanuel, God with Us! LOVE came down at Christmas to rescue and invite us to abide, to set captives free, give sight to the blind, and show us the way. Love came down at Christmas wrapped in swaddling clothes laying in a manger bed and rocked in a weary land so that we could have peace on earth.

Today is about celebrating, and so we celebrate. God has come to Us and demonstrated love for us most amazingly! If that isn't worth celebrating what is?

We celebrate the word becoming flesh and dwelt among us. "In the beginning was the word, and the word with God, and the word was God. He was in the beginning with God. All things come into being through him, and without Him, not one thing came into being. So, we celebrate the light that shines in darkness and the darkness did not overcome it.

Remember the:

Architect-Chief Cornerstone (1 Peter 2:6)

Artist-One altogether lovely (SoS 5:16)

Astronomer-sun and Morning Star (Revelation 5:16)

Baker-living Bread (John 6:35)

Biologist-life (John 14:6)

Good Shepherd (John 10)

Theologian-author and finisher of faith (Hebrews 12:2)

Emmanuel, Your love came down at Christmas. We celebrate you, absolute one. Thou who changest not, Abide with me!

— Rev. Dr. Dale Braxton

By Another Way

Matthew 2:1-12

And having been warned in a dream not to go back to Herod, they returned to their country by another route.
— *Matthew 2:12*

Gaslight–*To manipulate someone using psychological methods into questioning their own sanity or reasoning.*

Magi came to Herod asking where another King may be found, a sign in the sky directed them for directions. Herod attempts to gaslight the Magi into giving him information about the whereabouts of the newborn Jesus, saying he wants to worship too. They choose another way.

Sometimes, information we seek causes fear in people invested in the way things are and calls us to travel in ways not planned. Herod is terrified a rival is born, asks his astrologers for the place of the birth so that he can pay homage. Gaslighting. The visitors know better. A star, visit, gifts, and dream led the Magi to resist and go home another way.

Information can lead us home another way. They remind us that the way of presumed power and insincere adoration leads to paranoia and fake praise. We are called to travel another way, far from gaslighting rulers and worship the One in whom God has invested real and lasting power. We go by another way and find ourselves safely home.

God, help us recognize your voice and your word in all ways; lead us home by your way.

— Rev. Dr. LaTaunya M. Bynum

Greatness and Leadership

1 Corinthians 1:10

Now I appeal to you, brothers and sisters, by the name of our Lord Jesus Christ, that all of you be in agreement and that there be no divisions among you but that you be knit together in the same mind and the same purpose. — 1 Corinthians 1:10

Thanks to a gift from the Christian Church (Disciples of Christ) in Kansas, several in the neighboring Regions of Nebraska and Greater Kansas City received scholarships to participate in a series of workshops with the Kansas Leadership Center. KLC is founded on this principle: "anyone can lead, anytime, anywhere,"[1] and, "when everyone leads, the toughest challenges get seen and solved." We are encouraged to ask questions like these:

- "As you think about the future of____ , what is your *greatest* aspiration?"
- "As you think about the future of____, what is your *greatest* concern?"
- "What makes it hard to close the gap between those concerns and aspirations?"[2]

God, as You think about the future of the Body of Christ, what is Your greatest aspiration, Your greatest concern?

— Rev. William B. Rose-Heim

---

[1]Ed O'Malley & Julia Fabris McBride, When Everyone Leads: How the Toughest Challenges Get Seen and Solved, Bard Press, 2022, p.18, KLC Early Reader Edition.
[2]Ibid p.50

FOURTH DAY OF CHRISTMAS

He is Our Peace

Luke 2:8-20

So they hurried off and found Mary and Joseph, and the baby, who was lying in the manger.
— Luke 2:16

People occasionally ask, "Who arrived at Bethlehem first: the Magi or the Shepherds?" It is an honest question—our nativity scenes come with both sets of characters and many of us arrange them together when we decorate. Read literally, the Shepherds (Luke 2:8) came that night and the Magi (Matt. 2:1) came after several days of stargazing.

At a deeper level, the story of the Magi appears in the Gospel of Matthew. Matthew wrote for a Jewish Christian community that professed a continuity between the First Testament's witness to God's covenants with Israel and Judah and the coming of the Christ. However, Matthew is the Gospel writer who describes how pagan, astrologers from outside the covenant came as the first faithful responders to Christ's birth. Matthew also names four Gentile women in the genealogy of Jesus (Matthew 1:1-17; Tamar, Rahab, Ruth, and Bathsheba). Luke was a Gentile and wrote for a Gentile patron, Theophilus. In this most Gentile of gospels, the first people to respond to Jesus's birth are Jewish peasants.

The good news of Jesus Christ inspired these two evangelists to embrace people unlike themselves from the very beginning of their Gospels.

Newborn Savior, please help us embrace all people from the beginning that we met.

— Rev. Andy Mangum

He Is Our Peace (part 2)

Ephesians 2:11-22

[Jesus] came and preached peace to you who were far away and peace to those who were near.
— Ephesians 2:17

Fra Angelico's "The Visit of the Magi" that sits in the National Gallery in Washington, DC shows a stream of visitors arriving to pay homage to the Christ. In addition to the elaborately dressed visitors, the painters included some people dressed in rags. Some art historians surmise that these men represent people were excluded by society but who are included by Christ. Indeed, they stand on the remains of a broken-down wall (Ephesians 2:14).

The writer of Ephesians said of Christ, "He came and proclaimed peace to you who were far off and peace to those who were near" (2:17). The fuller reading of Ephesians 2:11-22 proclaims how Christ has formed a new undivided humanity, a singular household, founded on the testimony of prophets and apostles.

While historically and literarily the Magi and Shepherds have distinctly different visitations, they and the people they represent are united into one new humanity through Christ. Christ is our Peace. So, we who have claimed him as our Lord are called to be peacemakers in this world that continues to divide and exclude.

Prince of Peace, when the more we see division in our world, may we increase our making of peace.

— Rev. Andy Mangum

A Welcome Story

Matthew 2:13-15

When they had gone, an angel of the Lord appeared to Joseph in a dream. "Get up," he said, "take the child and his mother and escape to Egypt. Stay there until I tell you, for Herod is going to search for the child to kill him." So he got up, took the child and his mother during the night and left for Egypt, where he stayed until the death of Herod. And so was fulfilled what the Lord had said through the prophet: "Out of Egypt I called my son." — Matthew 2:13-15

In fear of persecution, they fled from Albania to New York, leaving their baby. Three sons later, the parents welcomed their older daughter. They owned a restaurant in a community where I pastored. This family, non-practicing Muslims, had never been inside a mosque or church, but I asked if we could host a "community" Christmas Eve service there. The father enthusiastically agreed even though he wasn't sure what that meant!

People gathered for scripture, candle-lighting, singing, prayer, and communion. The family each read part of the Christmas story and lit a candle. Their eyes got big, voice trembled; Mary and Joseph fleeing to Egypt became their story. As the father lit the Christ candle, a holy hush came over everyone. In awe, we knew God was in our midst. As this family experienced this story for the first time, we witnessed and experienced Jesus' birth in new and profound ways. Everyone partook in communion.

The story of God breaking into the world through the birth of a child, whom they called Jesus, Emmanuel, "God-With-Us," continues to be magical and mysterious.

We are grateful that Your story continues to speak to all of us who need to hear and be reminded that your presence is always amazing, breath-taking, and life-giving.

— Rev. Pamela Holt

35

As the Wheels Turn

Ezekiel 10:1-12

I looked, and I saw beside the cherubim four wheels, one beside each of the cherubim; the wheels sparkled like topaz. As for their appearance, the four of them looked alike; each was like a wheel intersecting a wheel. As they moved, they would go in any one of the four directions the cherubim faced; the wheels did not turn about as the cherubim went. The cherubim went in whatever direction the head faced, without turning as they went. Their entire bodies, including their backs, their hands and their wings, were completely full of eyes, as were their four wheels. — Ezekiel 9-12

This title may seem odd, relating to "*As the World Turns.*" Steering from secular to prophetic, look at Ezekiel 10. We have a front-row seat into the profound workings of the Angelic realm. This mystical passage invites us to look at the divinity, motion, and wheels of God's wonders at work. These beings are not merely in spiritual activity; they are ushering and abiding with the presence of God. These messengers and their wheels are God's helpers and movers of the Word and plan for our lives.

The jury may be out regarding your understanding of angels. Wherever you land, let the wheels of your imagination churn toward awe and wonder. Reflect upon the many times God provided unexplained assistance. This writing is never to challenge; it is a simple offering-a testimony to the numerous ways God takes great lengths to protect and reassure us that we can abide deeply within the beloved.

As the wheels of our lives turn, open ourselves to the next level of your plan. May we choose not to think over the where's, why's, and how's; help us focus on the fact that you are watching over your Word to ensure it is actively performing in our lives.

— Rev. Dr. Christal L. Williams

Journeying into the New Year

Ezra 7:1-10

On the first day of the first month the journey from Babylon
was begun....
— Ezra 7:9

After 70 years in exile, Jews were permitted to return to Jerusalem. Many decided to remain in diaspora communities established throughout the empire. Some, likely grandchildren and great-grandchildren – wanted to live in their ancestors' homeland. One group began their journey from Babylon to Jerusalem on the first day of the new year.

We often sense that the new year is perfect to do big things and make changes in our lives. Perhaps you have resolutions for these coming weeks. Whatever your plans, other things will arise too. May you navigate it all with persistence and grace.

I pray you sense in your life what seems clear in hindsight for Ezra. God was with them while they were in exile, providing comfort and hope. God was with them on the journey, nurturing dreams and protecting them. God was with them upon their return, as they rebuilt Jerusalem and rediscovered their heritage. May the promise of this season echo throughout this new year: Emmanuel, God with us.

Gracious God, help me to recognize your abiding presence in this new
year: through opportunities, challenges, surprises, doubts, heartaches,
joy, through everything.

— Rev. Joshua Patty

Moments to Movement

Acts 17:28

For in him we live and move and have our being.' As some of your own poets have said, "We are his offspring."
— Acts 17:28

I am excited about the New Year and daydream about gifts the months will unfold. Moving from one year to the next requires courage, reflection, and discernment around what stays in the previous year's chronicles, and what moves into next year's pile. Care, gratitude, and hope must ungird your travels. Don't allow residue of any bad situation, nor tensions from frayed human conditions, to move with you as it impedes your selfcare and overall growth. Refuse to get lost in misalignment. Allow God's beautiful joy, positivity, and creativity to be your driving force. This requires boldness. Be bold toward the love of God and the light of Christ!

God's grace and uninhibited optimism is there to navigate any circumstance. No one has it all figured out; view and move beyond current daily routine into a greater dimension of love and care. God has unlimited supplies of sincerity, humility, creativity, and deep love to help us freely walk the best pathway forward.

Sojourner, life offers a magnificent harvest, yielding more crops than we have room to receive. Move from the mundane to receiving the miracle of life itself.

You are the miracle found in moments of light and life, reminiscent of your unwavering love.

— Rev. Dr. Christal L. Williams

For Righteousness and Community

Matthew 3:13-17

Jesus replied, "Let it be so now; it is proper for us to do this to fulfill all righteousness." Then John consented.
— *Matthew 3:15*

Jesus was ready to begin his ministry and comes to John who is reluctant to perform the public act of repentance and submission for one whom he assigns ultimate worth. John does not feel worthy of being called a servant (3.11). But he hears Jesus say that being baptized is necessary for righteousness to be fulfilled.

Jesus' baptism is an invitation to righteousness – doing God's will in community.

- He and John act together to do the will of God.
- They perform the first public act of Jesus in humble obedience.
- God is pleased.

This is the way of Christmas and Epiphany – to see how Jesus responds in obedience to God as he says yes to God's call in his life and then for us to answer the call of God in our lives. We are called to live in community, humbly give ourselves to God, and follow the One who enters into life, goes beyond death, and invites us to enter the baptismal waters and to rise and follow him.

God, may we hear your voice reminding us to follow humbly and completely.

— Rev. Dr. LaTaunya M. Bynum

A Christmas Reading

John 1:1-5

In the beginning was the Word, and the Word was with God, and the Word was God. He was with God in the beginning. Through him all things were made; without him nothing was made that has been made. In him was life, and that life was the light of all mankind. The light shines in the darkness, and the darkness has not overcome it. — John 1:1-5

John 1 reflects Genesis 1, where humanity started "in the beginning." It presents Jesus Christ as "the *Word,* or *Logos*, who was there in the beginning." John bore witness to the light. He came to prepare the way for Jesus to be revealed and sheds light on his purpose.

Jesus came into a world that didn't notice he was the Messiah. Can you imagine waiting on the Messiah to come, and then failing to recognize him when he shows up? In the midst of gatherings, presents, and decorations, we may miss the birth that all the fuss is about.

In celebrating his birth, we have an invitation to become children of God. *"To all who received him, he gave power to become children of God, who were born, not of blood, but of God."* While the law came through Moses, *"grace and truth came through Jesus Christ."* What the law could not do, grace and truth did – opening the doors to life through not only his birth, but through his sacrificial death.

We thank you for the invitation to receive baby Jesus in our hearts, destined with intention and purpose to love us unconditionally, giving hope for life on earth as in heaven.

— Rev. Dr. Nadine Burton

Can I Get a Witness?

Psalm 63:1-8

You, God, are my God,
earnestly I seek you;
I thirst for you,
my whole being longs for you,
in a dry and parched land
where there is no water.
— Psalm 63:1

My title's question is not asked in Ps 63, yet the psalmist's cry answers it, and urges us to cry the same: "O God! You are the One I seek."

Standing at the beginning of another year, isn't David's cry ours as well, as people of faith? In a desperate time, in a lonely, starved, and thirsty time, the psalmist remembers to whom he belongs-the One whose love is better than life itself. The poet rejoices, lifts hands in praise and sings out, "I will bless you as long as I live!" It's an affirmation of faith! Without knowing all that lies ahead, his song affirms that life with God is a feast like none other, that only God can sustain his life. How can our song be otherwise?

What better words than these to reaffirm our faith and guide us into the new year God has given: *"O God, you are my God." Because your love is better than life, my lips will glorify you. And so I bless you while I live; in your Name I lift up my hands."*

May your love keep us faithful until our life becomes more yours than ours—servants of a servant Church in Christ's name.

— Rev. Katherine Kinnamon

ESPERANZA

Esperanza en camino

"Que el Dios de la esperanza os llene de toda alegría y paz al confiar en él, para que podáis rebosar de esperanza por el poder del Espíritu Santo".
— Romanos 15:13

Hace años, mientras vivía en la ciudad de Nueva York, recibí la visita de un pastor de Guatemala. Como es costumbre en la cultura hispana, llegó con regalos para mí como su anfitriona y para sus amigos. El pastor me dio lo que parecía un mini telar hecho con piezas de madera rústicas. El telar sostenía un pequeño tapiz de hilo hecho por las mujeres indígenas locales en un pueblo de Guatemala. Los colores y el diseño eran hermosos, pero lo que más me llamó la atención fue el mensaje que la tejedora había creado y capturado para siempre en ese tapiz: "Esperanza en camino."

Las mujeres del pueblo habían aprendido del evangelio durante las clases bíblicas, y lo que capturaron es el mejor anuncio del evangelio y el mejor mensaje de adviento que jamás había recibido. Para los pobladores guatemaltecos, Esperanza en camino significaba todo. ¡Dios está en camino, Jesús viene, el Espíritu Santo no se demorará! Esperanza en camino, cuando la vida es difícil, cuando la comida es escasa, cuando nuestro hogar está en ruinas, cuando nuestras relaciones están rotas. Esperanza en camino, es la palabra de Dios que dirige nuestros pasos en la noche. Esperanza en camino es luz en nuestra hora más oscura y bálsamo para nuestro dolor. Esperanza en camino, es esperanza contra esperanza de que todo estará bien, es la esperanza de que este mundo será mejor porque contra las condiciones de mi entorno o detalles de mi situación, hay un Dios que me ama tanto que ha enviado a su hijo por mí! Hasta el día de hoy guardo ese tapiz rústico en mi oficina, un recordatorio de la fe en el más simple de los mensajes. ¡El Adviento es un recordatorio de que la esperanza está en camino!

Querido Dios, estamos agradecidos por el mayor de los regalos durante esta temporada de Adviento, tu hijo Jesús. No olvidemos que Él es la esperanza de este mundo y la esperanza de nuestras vidas. Que a aquellos que se sienten desesperados hoy se les recuerde que la esperanza está en camino. Amén.

HOPE

Romans 15:13

May the God of hope fill you with all joy and peace as you trust in him, so that you may overflow with hope by the power of the Holy Spirit.
— Romans 15:13

I hosted a pastor from Guatemala, and is customary in Hispanic culture, he arrived with gifts-a mini-weaving loom made with rustic wooden pieces holding a small yarn tapestry made by local indigenous women. The colors and design were beautiful; what struck me most was the message captured forever: "Esperanza en camino;" Hope is on its way.

For the Guatemalan villagers, Esperanza en camino meant all-God is on his way, Jesus is coming, Holy Spirit will not delay! When life is difficult, food sparse, our home in shambles, relationships are broken, Esperanza en camino, directs our steps in the night. Esperanza en camino is light in our darkest hour and balm to our sorrow, is hope that all will be right and that this world will be better because against the conditions of my surroundings or details of my situation, God loves me so much that he sent his son for me! Advent is a reminder that hope is on its way!

Dear God, as we light our first candle, we are thankful for the greatest gift during this advent season, your son Jesus-our hope of this world and our lives. May those who feel hopeless be reminded that hope is on its way.

— Rev. Evangelina "Vangie" Perez

PAZ

Cuando pasares por las aguas,
yo seré contigo;
y por los ríos, no te anegarán
Cuando pasares por el fuego,
no te quemarás,
ni la llama arderá en ti.
— Isaías 43:2

"Padre, no sé qué enfrentaré hoy, qué noticias recibiré o qué desafíos se me presentarán, pero sé que todo estará bien cuando enfrente todas las cosas contigo." Así es como termino mi oración por las mañanas, y me ha ayudado a vivir dentro de dos realidades.

La primera es que mi vida puede cambiar en cualquier momento. Un mensaje de texto, correo electrónico o llamada inesperada puede cambiar mi día, estado de ánimo o mi vida; después de todo, como dice Santiago 4:14, *"no saben lo que traerá el mañana, y nuestra vida no es más que neblina".*

La segunda realidad es que no importa las noticias o los desafíos que enfrente, cuando los enfrente con Dios, todo estará bien. Isaías 43:2 me recuerda que Dios está con nosotros, y porque Él está con nosotros, los ríos, no nos abrumarán, ni las llamas nos consumirán. Saber que no estoy solo me da la paz necesaria para enfrentar todos los días.

Tal vez como yo, has recibido noticias que te han cambiado la vida y te han sacudido hasta la médula y te han cambiado. Recordemos que todo estará bien gracias a Emmanuel. Como escribió el salmista, *"puedes acostarte y dormir en paz porque solo el Señor nos hace sentir confiados."* Salmo 4:8

Señor, mientras encendemos la vela de la paz, danos paz recordándonos
que todo estará bien, porque tú estás con nosotros.

PEACE

When you pass through the waters,
I will be with you;
and when you pass through the rivers,
they will not sweep over you.
When you walk through the fire,
you will not be burned;
the flames will not set you ablaze.
— *Isaiah 43:2*

"Father, I don't know what I will face today, what news I will receive, or what challenges will come my way, but I know that everything will be okay when I face all things with you." That is how I end my morning prayer, and it helps me live into two realities.

First is that my life can change at any moment. An unexpected text, email, or call can change my day, mood, or life. "You do not know what tomorrow will bring, and our life is but a vapor." James 4:14

The second reality is that no matter the news or the challenges, when I face them with God everything will be okay. Isaiah 43:2 reminds that God is with us, and because he is with us, the rivers, will not overwhelm us, nor the flames consume us. Knowing that I am not alone gives the peace needed to face every day.

Perhaps you have received life-changing news that shakes you to your core and changed you. Everything will be okay because of Emmanuel. "You can lie down and sleep in peace because the Lord alone will keep you safe." Psalm 4:8

Lord, as we light the candle of peace, give us peace reminding that everything is okay, for you are with us.

— Rev. Samuel Ramirez

AMOR

"Por tanto, el mismo Señor les dará la señal: He aquí que la virgen concebirá y dará a luz un hijo, y llamará su nombre Emanuel."
— *Isaías 7:14 RVA*

El mensaje del Evangelio más conocido de las Escrituras puede muy bien ser Juan 3:16 en el que establece claramente la razón profunda y fundamental de la venida de Dios a la humanidad. "Porque de tal manera amó Dios al mundo". Si Dios con nosotros esta, es por el amor de Dios.

Una forma en que podríamos tener una idea de lo que es esto, es cuando nos damos cuenta de que debería haber una razón fundamental por la que estaríamos dispuestos a hacer algo por otra persona que puede no estar muy cómodo para uno. ¿Sería por amor? Cuando hacemos algo para el beneficio de otra persona, y hacerlo es bastante incómodo, debemos reflexionar sobre el por qué estamos dispuestos a sentirnos incómodos para el beneficio de otra persona. ¿Cuál sería la verdadera razón para que lo hiciéramos? ¡Porque Dios nos amó tanto! Se necesitó la llegada de este tipo de amor, y hacerlo por nosotros significaba dejar Su lugar de gloria, convertirse en un siervo, capaz de sentir el dolor humano, el hambre, la sed y la muerte. ¿Es nuestro amor por nuestro prójimo tan grande que estamos dispuestos a sentirnos inusualmente incómodos para los demás? Emanuel, Dios se hizo carne por amor. El amor hace la diferencia. Vivamos amor.

Oración: *Oh Señor Jesucristo, ayúdanos a estar dispuestos a sentirnos incómodos simplemente por amor. En el Nombre de Jesús oramos.*

LOVE

"Therefore the Lord himself will give you a sign. Look, the young woman is with child and shall bear a son and shall name him Immanuel."
— Isaiah 7:14 NRSVUE

The most well-known Gospel message may be John 3:16; the profound and fundamental reason for God coming to humanity, *"For God so loved the World."*

We might have an idea of what this is when we realize that there should be a fundamental reason why we would be willing to do something for someone else that may not be very comfortable. Would it be because of love? When we do something for someone else, and doing so is uncomfortable, we should reflect on why we are willing to be uncomfortable for someone else's benefit. What would be the reason?

Because God loved us! It took this kind of love to come, and doing so meant leaving His place of glory, becoming a servant, feeling human pain, hunger, thirst, and death. Is our love for our neighbor so, that we are willing to be unusually uncomfortable for others? Immanuel, God became flesh because of love. Love makes a difference. Live love.

Oh Lord Jesus Christ, as we light our third candle this Advent, help us to be willing to be uncomfortable simply because of love.

— Rev. Xosé Escamilla

GOZO

Filipenses 4:4-9

Gozaos en el Señor siempre: otra vez digo: Que os gocéis.
— Filipenses 4:4

El gozo es una teoría desde adentro hacia fuera. Tal vez no tiene sentido esto, pero es vivido en relación con Jesús a través del Espíritu. Uno primero debe entender que el gozo y la felicidad no son lo mismo. Uno es desde afuera hacia dentro, mientras el otro es desde adentro hacia fuera. Es como Jesús durante su ministerio que fue desde afuera hacia dentro, y en el Cristo resucitado se convirtió en desde adentro hacia fuera por el Espíritu.

Aquello que es desde afuera hacia dentro opera en lo externo e impacta lo interno. Puedes sentirte feliz y alguien hace o dice algo y esa felicidad se convierta en tristeza, enojo o frustración. Lo que paso externamente cambio lo que sentiste en lo interno.

Pero el gozo es lo inverso. Vive en lo interno e impacta lo externo. Vez, no es dependiente de las circunstancias externas porque viene de Cristo a través del Espíritu. Puedes tener un mal día, una experiencia o dificultad y aún sentir gozo. Te nutrirá internamente y te ayudará a navegar lo externo de maneras que impactan lo que te rodea. ¡Es contagioso!

Esto es el verdadero gozo y aunque tal vez no tiene sentido, es como Jesús entregando su vida en la cruz por nosotros, el gozo también se trata del amor de Dios por el mundo.

Oración: Espíritu Santo, mientras encendemos la vela del gozo, que la experiencia interna del gozo fluya dentro de nosotros para que podamos continuar la obra de compartir el gozo de Cristo externamente al mundo.

JOY

Philippians 4:4-9

Rejoice in the Lord always. I will say it again: Rejoice!
— Philippians 4:4

Joy is inside-out. That may not make sense, but it is lived in relationship with Jesus through the Spirit. Joy and happiness aren't the same. One is outside-in; the other inside-out. It's like Jesus during his ministry who was outside-in, and in the resurrected Christ became inside-out through the Spirit.

That which is outside-in happens in the external and impacts the internal. You can be feeling happy, and someone does or says something that takes happy to sad, mad or frustrating. What happened externally changed how you feel internally.

Joy is the inverse. It lives internally and impacts the external. Joy isn't dependent on external circumstances because it comes from Christ through the Spirit. You can have a bad day, hardship, or difficulty and still feel joy. It nourishes you internally and helps you navigate the external in ways that impact your surroundings. It's contagious!

This is true joy and while it might not make sense, it's like Jesus giving his life on the cross for us, it too is about God's love for the world.

Holy Spirit, as we light the candle of Joy, may the internal experience of joy flow alive within us so we may continue the work of sharing the joy of Christ externally to the world.

— Rev. Lori Tapia

CRISTO

Isaías 9:2

El pueblo que andaba en tinieblas vio gran luz; los que moraban en tierra de sombra de muerte, luz resplandeció sobre ellos.
— *Isaías 9:2*

Cuando la luz brilla en las tinieblas, tenemos dos opciones. Podemos cerrar y apretar los ojos, levantar la sabana sobre la cabeza, y pelear para que no entre la luz. O, podemos despertar a ella. La luz de Jesús que irrumpe en el mundo vino para despertarnos. Vino para realizar la jubilosa anticipación, la completa paz, el abundante gozo, y el inagotable amor que tanto necesitábamos y anhelábamos.

¡La luz resplandeció! ¡La salvación llegó!

Porque un niño nos es nacido, hijo nos es dado!

Darse cuenta de esta realidad, y de la vida que le acompaña, require una respuesta. Podemos tratar de escondernos de la luz, cerrar nuestros ojos e ignorarla... o podemos abrazarla, deleitarnos en su resplandor, y regocijarnos en su bondad.

Encendemos la vela de Cristo. Nos regocijamos en la luz que brilla en la oscuridad y declaramos con alabanza -

¡Al mundo paz, nació Jesús! ¡Aleluya!

Padre de las luces, quien da todo lo que es bueno y perfecto, te damos gracias por el regalo de tu Hijo, Jesús, la Luz del mundo. Permite que despertemos a Su luz y que seamos portadores de ella. Por tu Espíritu oramos, en el nombre de Jesús, Amén.

CHRIST

Isaiah 9:2

The people walking in darkness have seen a great light;
on those living in the land of deep darkness a light has dawned.
— Isaiah 9:2

When light shines through the darkness, we can squint and squeeze our eyes, pull back the cover over our heads, and block out the light. Or, we can awaken to it. The in-breaking light of Jesus came to awaken us. He came to fulfill the joyful hope, abundant peace, exuberant joy, and never-ending love we so desperately needed and longed for.

Becoming aware of this reality, and the life that comes with it, requires a response. We can try to hide from the light, close our eyes and ignore it... or we can embrace it, delight in its radiance, and rejoice in its goodness.

We light the Christ candle as we rejoice in the light that shines in the darkness and declare with praise - Joy to the world! The Lord has come!

Father of lights, who gives every good and perfect gift, we thank you for gift of your Son, Jesus, the Light of the world. May we be awakened to the light and may we be bearers of it.

— Rev. Iván Santiago and Rev. Milca Rivera

CONTRIBUTORS

Rev. Thaddaeus B. Allen is the Regional Minister for the West Virginia, Pennsylvania, and Northeastern regions.

Rev. Dr. Denise Bell is the former Regional Minister for the Georgia region.

Rev. Dr. Dale Braxton is the Acting Regional Minister for the Alabama/Northwest Florida region.

Rev. Dr. Nadine Burton is the Executive Regional Minister for the Great River region.

Rev. Dr. LaTaunya M. Bynum is the Regional Minister for the Northern California-Nevada region.

Rev. Dr. Teresa Dulyea-Parker is the retired Regional Minister and President for the Illinois and Wisconsin and Michigan regions.

Rev. Xosé Escamilla is Senior Pastor of Casa de Oración in San Diego, California.

Rev. Dr. Don K. Gillett II is the Regional Minister for the Kentucky region.

Rev. Allen V. Harris is the Regional Pastor & President for the Ohio region.

Rev. Dr. Jay R. Hartley is the Regional Minister and President for the Arizona region.

Rev. Pam Holt is the Regional Minister for the Oklahoma region.

Rev. Dr. Eugene James is the retired Regional Minister for the Michigan region.

Rev. Katherine Kinnamon is an Associate Regional Minister for the Mid-America region.

Rev. Dr. Paul Koch is a Regional Minister for the Mid-America region.

Rev. Cheryl Russell Kunkel is an Associate Regional Minister for the Indiana region.

Rev. Jennifer Long is an Associate Regional Minister for the Mid-America region.

Rev. Andy Mangum is the Regional Minister and President in the Southwest region.

Rev. Ken Marston is the Co-Regional Minister in the Kansas region.

Rev. Sandy Messick is the Regional Minister in the Florida region.

Rev. Christopher B. Morton is the Regional Minister in the Nebraska region.

Rev. Teresa "Terri" Hord Owens is the General Minister and President of the Christian Church (Disciples of Christ) in the United States and Canada.

Rev. Joshua Patty is the Regional Minister the Upper Midwest region.

Rev. Evangelina "Vangie" Perez is the Moderator of the National Hispanic and Bilingual Fellowship and Hispanic Board and Pastor of Iglesia Cristiana Kayros, Arlington, Texas.

Rev. Samuel Ramirez is the Past Moderator of Obra Hispana and Pastor of Sun Valley Church.

Rev. Milca Rivera is President of the National Hispanic and Bilingual Women's Ministry Representative in Obra Hispana and co-pastor of Iglesia Cristiana (Discípulos de Cristo), Deltona, Florida.

Rev. Bill Robey is the Interim Regional Minister in the Northern Lights region.

Rev. William B. Rose-Heim is the Regional Minister and President in Greater Kansas City region.

Rev. Ron Routledge is a Regional Minister in the Mid-America region.

Rev. Iván Santiago is the Men's Co-Representative in Obra Hispana and co-pastor of Iglesia Cristiana (Discípulos de Cristo), Deltona, Florida.

Rev. Molly Smothers is an Associate Regional Minister in the Kentucky region.

Rev. Dr. Phil Snider is an Associate Regional Minister in the Mid-America region.

Rev. Tom Stanley is the Co-Regional Minister in the Kansas region.

Rev. Lori Tapia is National Pastor for the Central Pastoral Office for Hispanic Ministries, Obra Hispana

Rev. Dr. Christal L. Williams is the Regional Minister & President in the Tennessee region.

Rev. David Woodard is an Associate Regional Minister in the Mid-America region.